insight from experts series

D0925986

303

Solutions
for
Boosting Creativity
& Solving Challenges

Compiled by
Doug Smart

James & Brookfield
J&B
Publishers

Book Designer: Paula Chance
Copyright © 2005

Disclaimer: This book is a compilation of ideas from numerous experts.
As such, the views expressed are those of the authors
and not necessarily the views of James & Brookfield Publishers.

For more information, contact:
James & Brookfield Publishers
P.O. Box 768024
Roswell, GA 30076

ISBN 0-9771912-5-7
Library of Congress Cataloging in Publication Data
10 9 8 7 6 5 4 3 2 1

"The marble not yet carved can hold the form of every thought the greatest artist has."

— Michelangelo

1. **Expand your brain power by joining a mastermind group.** Such groups meet on a regular basis, and through collective thinking, they generate ideas to help solve challenges the members are facing.

— Donna Satchell

2. **Forget about perfectionism.** It's overrated!

— Mandi Stanley

3. **A life without challenges is like playing golf at night.** You have no idea where your ball is going, therefore you have no way of keeping score.

— David G. Lewis

4. **Use the ABC's:** *attitude, behavior* and *controlled breathing* **to help clear your mind of stress and negative attitudes, all of which can block creativity.**

— *Cheryl Stock*

5. **Beware of what you already know.** That knowledge might turn out to be an obstacle to seeing what else is possible.

— *Phoebe Bailey*

6. **Be C.R.E.A.T.I.V.E.:** *Confident, Resourceful, Enthused, Aspiring, Talented, Inspiring, Vibrant* **and** *Empowered!*

— *Keith L. Brown*

7. **Most people fall into a creative slump at least once a year.** It is a time when we feel tired, worn out and as if we have nothing creative to offer. All of us get our elastics stretched.

— Linda Edgecombe

8. **Use your mind as your mallet to overcome your challenges.** They may seem to present themselves as a brick wall. Strengthen your mind and make it your mallet. Use it to knock down your wall brick by brick by brick!

— Kafi Matimiloju

9. **Make creativity the fuel that makes you go.**

— DJ Harrington

10. **Draw on your past experiences to solve the problems of today.** You have met many challenges to get where you are. Review what has worked for you and capitalize on your strengths.

— *Mike Monahan*

11. **"All or nothing" thinking closes the mind to what might really be possible.**

— *Sid Ridgley*

12. **Good ideas and creative input must come from all levels of the organization, or the organization will wither.**

— *Greg Maciolek*

13. **Creative minds have no limits.**

— *Robert Stack*

14. **Prepare your mind.** In today's complex business world, the ability to make quick, informed decisions is a critical asset.

— Connie Dieken

15. **Avoid "can't do" thinking.** That type of negative thinking blocks creative problem-solving. Choose to focus on "possibility thinking."

— Donna Satchell

16. **Surrender the inclination to have everything lined up before acting, or you will find it very difficult to get started on new projects.** Practice improvising and being spontaneous.

— Phoebe Bailey

17. **When your approach to a problem reaches a point in which nothing seems to be working, you are experiencing a stalemate.** A stalemate does not mean the problem is unsolvable. Some effective approaches for a stalemate include:

- *Taking a break.* Sometimes just some distance in time and space will spawn new ideas, approaches and solutions.

- *Asking for someone else's opinions and assistance.*

— Mike Monahan

18. **Typically, a new idea gets its first negative response within 3 seconds**, such as "that won't work, we don't have the budget, we tried that already, etc."

— Doug Smart

19. For lots of people, jigsaw puzzles are a fun way to stimulate their minds for creativity. **Puzzles help us activate parts of our brain less frequently used, which can help us think in fresh ways.** Researchers even recommend puzzles as a way to help us stay mentally young.

— *Cheryl Stock*

20. **When people participate through healthy dialogue, creativity and commitment increase.**

— *Sid Ridgley*

21. **Be unique!** After all, you were born an original, so why live as a copy!

— *Keith L. Brown*

22. **Don't blame others for your current situation.** With the exception of disease and disaster, our current state is generally the result of our own actions and decisions. If you don't like where you are or what you are doing, change it.

— *Mike Monahan*

23. **Creativity comes when you are stimulated, focused and engaged.**

— *Robert Stack*

24. **Don't label challenges – describe them.** When you focus on clearly describing a problem, the solutions will follow.

— *Connie Dieken*

25. **Face your challenges head on and avoid self-derailment.** When a challenge stares you in the face, stand firm and be ready for the freight train that is heading your way. Someone or something will always try and derail you, so invest your time in building yourself up and avoid knocking yourself down.

— Kafi Matimiloju

26. **Lack of imagination is nothing more than a lack of creative problem solving skills.**

— David G. Lewis

27. **Imagination exercises the mind.**
— *Kafi Matimiloju*

28. **Go and do something new to give your creativity a jolt.** Suggestions include: start immediately on something you have not done yet, go back to school, take an art class even if you think you are not artsy, learn to play an instrument, go camping by yourself and build your own fire for roasting marshmallows, write, sing, and act.
— *Linda Edgecombe*

29. **The more you plan, the easier it is to execute any kind of plan.**
— *Greg Maciolek*

30. **A pinch of fun doesn't hurt.**

— *DJ Harrington*

31. **Boost creativity by "thinking green."** For example, spend time outside, grow a plant in your office, or use a green screensaver.

— *Mandi Stanley*

32. **Understand when you are most creative and plan accordingly**. Morning, afternoon or evening – which is best for *your* creativity? Set aside the appropriate time of day to engage in your creative pursuits.

— *Donna Satchell*

33. **Writing your thoughts at the end of the day is a great stress releaser and allows you to sleep better.**

— Linda Edgecombe

34. **Go to bed on time.** Nothing boosts creative energy as well as a good night's sleep.

— Mandi Stanley

35. Our subconscious minds work all the time, even when sleeping. **A great creativity tool and timesaver is to frame a problem and sleep on it!** While you are sleeping, your subconscious mind will work on solutions. When you awake, be prepared to record the exciting and creative ideas that come to mind.

— Mike Monahan

36. **Create a team committed to important values.**

— Phoebe Bailey

37. **Making tough decisions is much easier when you know what your values are.**

— Sid Ridgley

38. **Brainstorming gives your mind a great workout without judgments being made as to the quality of the ideas.** That frees you to think of outrageous new solutions.

— Linda Edgecombe

39. **Credibility is the cornerstone of creativity.** Credibility boosts creativity by encouraging trust, initiative, and productive risk-taking.

— Connie Dieken

40. **When was the last time you did something for the first time?**

— Keith L. Brown

41. **Stimulate your creative thinking by considering how to reverse or rearrange part of the item to create a different item.** An example would be a reversible jacket.

— Donna Satchell

42. **Creativity requires discipline in order to feel free to be creative.** Here is a time management suggestion. Make a list of what you want or need to accomplish in order to make your dreams come true. Incorporate those items with your regular "to do" lists for the day, week, month and year.

— *Doug Smart*

43. **Freedom inhibits creativity.** There are nothing like restrictions to get you thinking. For example, if you're stuck for an idea, open a dictionary or any book and randomly select a word; formulate ideas incorporating this word. You'll be surprised how well this works at breaking mental log jams.

— *Linda Edgecombe*

44. **It is critical for owners, senior execs, and managers at all levels to create an environment where workers excel, where employees actually look forward to coming to work and practically have to be told they have to go home at the end of the day!** That is an ideal environment.

— *Greg Maciolek*

45. **When thinking about launching a new process, get front line input first.**

— *Sid Ridgley*

46. **Fix the problem, not the blame.**

— *Mandi Stanley*

47. **When group members begin to focus on similarities instead of differences, it encourages the open flow of creativity.**

— *David G. Lewis*

48. The I's have it. **Do some *informational interviewing* to gather *ideas for imaginative, ingenious, and innovative solutions to challenges.*** Ask others for two suggestions on how they might handle a particular situation. Often, their insight will trigger new ideas and solutions in your mind.

— Cheryl Stock

49. **Have a Plan B.** In an ideal world, everything is perfect and goes according to plan. When faced with an expected challenge, be prepared to execute your Plan B and put it into action. Work your backup plan and overcome your challenge with a vengeance.

— Kafi Matimiloju

50. **Look at stress as a creative ingredient to success**.

— *DJ Harrington*

51. **Imagine yourself in another person's position and address a challenge from their perspective.** For example, ask yourself, "How would so-and-so handle this?" You don't have to do what that person would do, but it might open up your thinking to fresh possibilities by imagining how someone else would respond.

— *Donna Satchell*

52. **To solve a problem, make it fun.**
— Robert Stack

53. Develop your sense of humor. Tell jokes and make funny observations, sign up for a comedy class, go to an improv performance or rent funny movies. **Humor restores us when we feel creatively challenged.**
— Cheryl Stock

54. **Coach others to take their strengths to extraordinary heights.** This is a better strategy than coaching them to bring their weaknesses up to mediocre.
— Greg Maciolek

55. **Create a cheer or chant for your team.**
Here is a team chant that has motivated
thousands and continues to do so:

GOOD JOB!

Good Job! (Pause) GOOD JOB!

Good Job! (Pause) G-Double O-D-J-O-B!
GOOD JOB!

Good JOB!

— Keith L. Brown

56. Consider life as a game. **The challenges we
encounter are God's gifts to keep us in a
mindset of creativity.**

— Phoebe Bailey

57. **Avoid negative self-talk as it gets in the
way of being able to think clearly.**

— Sid Ridgley

58. **Learn to discern the differences between important and urgent.** Chasing urgency creates fatigue and poor decisions. Not everything important is urgent and not everything urgent is important. You can set boundaries by learning to say "no."

— *Mike Monahan*

59. **When faced with a challenge, tap into your greatest resource — other people**! Invest wisely in your resources and establish a board of directors or mastermind group. When faced with a major roadblock, use your group to brainstorm solutions and help you think outside the box.

— *Kafi Matimiloju*

60. **Every night before bedtime, think of one thing you're grateful for that you have never been grateful for before.**

— Mandi Stanley

61. **A grateful heart is a light heart.**
A resentful heart is a heavy heart.

— Doug Smart

62. **To open up your creativity, you have to be vulnerable by being willing to risk losing something.**

— David G. Lewis

63. **Learn to brainstorm in groups of diverse talents and experiences.** No one is allowed to say, "Oh, that will never work!"

— Phoebe Bailey

64. **Never underestimate the power of working in a small group.** The dynamics of working with others not only increases the level of creativity that takes place, it decreases stress, too.

— David G. Lewis

65. **Help everyone on the team understand the objectives so all will think and work as a supportive team.** When people feel closer to the center, they're more creative and nurturing.

— Connie Dieken

66. **Teams are strengthened through shared experiences of winning, losing, playing, and learning together.**

— Sid Ridgley

67. **To increase team creativity, hold brainstorming meetings in new locations.** Many times the sameness of a location dulls creative thinking. New places – such as in a park, at the beach, or in a restaurant, with their different sounds, sights, and smells, can help generate new ideas.

— Donna Satchell

68. **There is a strong correlation between high involvement of team members in the work process—making them feel like co-owners—and high productivity and low absenteeism.**

— Greg Maciolek

69. **Schedule intermittent celebrations to keep project teams energized.** Creativity thrives in play.

— Phoebe Bailey

70. **It's time to have an "I Can't *Fun*eral."** Give each team member an index card and have them describe the biggest obstacle holding them back (example: "I can't change my attitude."). Have a few volunteers read theirs aloud. Then get a large casket (garbage pail) and have all the cards thrown into it. Deliver a brief comment like this, "Herein lies 'I can't.' 'I can't' is survived by the relatives 'I can,' 'I will,' 'I must.' We bury 'I can't' today and birth teamwork and greatness!"

— Keith L. Brown

71. Capture your creative thoughts in a notebook. You may discover about ninety percent of your ideas aren't worth a thing. Don't worry, that's normal. **What's important are the ten percent that are brilliant.**

— Linda Edgecombe

72. **Creative idea: Think about how to eliminate a part or ingredient in order to create an improved item.** An example would be fat-free potato chips.

— Donna Satchell

73. **Connect the dots between two columns of related but unconnected items as an exercise that can help you think differently about problems and their solutions.**

— Cheryl Stock

74. **How many people have been bitten by an elephant? Remember it's the small things, not the big ones, that bite you.**
— *DJ Harrington*

75. **You can't drive without gas in the tank.** Read everything possible. Spark conversations. Stay current and connected and you'll rev your own engine.
— *Connie Dieken*

76. **Analyze the messages you are giving yourself.** Negative self-talk can be insidious and defeating. Admit your mistakes but concentrate on your competencies. Convince yourself you can do better next time.
— *Mike Monahan*

77. Be willing to explore and be adventuresome. **If you already know, you are not creating anything.**

— Phoebe Bailey

78. **Clutter cripples creativity.** When there is too much "stuff" around, it is difficult to keep from being distracted by the visual burden of it all. Clean up and clear out clutter so you can concentrate and create creative bursts!

— Cheryl Stock

79. In education today, all school districts across the United States monitor AYP, *Adequate Yearly Progress.* As I empower educators and students nationwide, I encourage them to transform *Adequate Yearly Progress* into *All Youth Prosper!* **We can do much better than focusing on adequate!**

— *Keith L. Brown*

80. **Challenges are opportunities to change and grow.**

— *Robert Stack*

81. Endless "to do" lists are the source of many challenges. **Consider making a "have done" list so you can see your progress.**

— *Mandi Stanley*

82. **Overcoming a challenge takes acceptance, persistence and motivation.**

— Kafi Matimiloju

83. **Thoughts, combined with actions, can change the world. But a thought alone is simply a thought.**

— Sid Ridgley

84. **The biggest waste I see in most companies is under utilized creativity of the people who work there.** Remember that the employees *are* the company. Strategically, they are the company's competitive advantage.

— Greg Maciolek

85. Not all problems are of equal importance or urgency. **Prioritize your challenges!**
— Mike Monahan

86. **Know your boiling point.** When creativity comes to a screeching halt, recognize your body's hint. Take a temporary break to re-energize and get back on point.
— Connie Dieken

87. People in your local community and family will always remember your past failures and remind you of them. **Smile, ignore their out-dated perceptions, and succeed anyway!**
— David G. Lewis

88. **When the going gets tough, learn to ask for help.**

— Robert Stack

89. **Your earnings are tied to your "learnings."** To earn more, learn more.

— Doug Smart

90. **Be a well-rounded reader.** Individuals who are well-read have more information which they can draw upon when addressing challenges.

— Donna Satchell

91. Read as much as you can about everything that interests you. **Books exercise your brain, provide inspiration and fill you with information that allows you to make creative connections easily.**

— Linda Edgecombe

92. **Voracious readers see what's coming around the corner and are more adaptable.**

— Connie Dieken

93. **Expand your mental capacity by learning something new each day, such as a word, a fact of history, or a song.**

— Phoebe Bailey

94. **Don't limit your reading sessions to "bathroom time."**

— DJ Harrington

95. **Try turning off your TV for a week.** It's tough, but you'll be amazed how the stress in your home decreases, you read more and get more sleep. What else can you do with all this time on your hands?

— *Linda Edgecombe*

96. **Problems exist and have consequences regardless of whether you acknowledge them or not.** Just because you aren't aware of a problem doesn't mean it isn't real. For example, if you have high cholesterol but haven't had your cholesterol checked, you still have high cholesterol. The same is true for relationship and business problems. Active inquiry and measurement of processes and outcomes are necessary to identify problems.

— *Mike Monahan*

97. **Devote time every month to on-going strategic problem solving.**

— Greg Maciolek

98. **When dealing with multiple challenges, choose one and get it done.**

— Robert Stack

99. **Solve daily challenges and reduce stress simultaneously by having backups:** an extra house key hidden well, extra stamps, an emergency $20 bill in your car – even an extra diaper in your glove compartment!

— Mandi Stanley

100. **Everything in life requires some kind of risk.** To risk nothing is to gain nothing.

— David G. Lewis

101. **One smart strategy for risk management is to ask yourself, "What is the worst that can happen?"** If the answer is something you can easily live with, the risk is obviously minimal. If the worst case would cause you some harm, you need to think carefully before deciding. If the worst case would be devastating to you, don't take the risk.

— *Cheryl Stock*

102. **Attack problems and challenges immediately.** They rarely go away and can get worse quickly. When problems arise, deal with them as soon as you can and then get back on track with the task at hand.

— *Kafi Matimiloju*

103. **The first step to solving a challenge is to take action.**

— *David G. Lewis*

104. **Get up on time so you can start your day unrushed.**

— *Mandi Stanley*

105. **I always work under the assumption that employees *want* to make a difference by contributing.** A leader's job is to let them do that.

— *Greg Maciolek*

106. **Establish a culture of approval.** Idea production rises dramatically when people know it's okay to voice imperfect thoughts and ideas as part of the solution-seeking process. They walk away feeling pleased with making worthwhile contributions.

— *Connie Dieken*

107. **Define your problem.** Grab a sheet of paper, electronic notebook, computer or whatever you use to make notes, and define your problem in detail. You'll probably find ideas positively spewing out once you've done this.

— Linda Edgecombe

108. **Embrace challenges as pathways to feelings of exhilaration.**

— Sid Ridgley

109. **Go toward what you want as opposed to always going away from what you don't want.** Chose to be motivated by a reward rather than by avoidance of pain. When you choose a positive direction, you are more likely to get what you want.

— Mike Monahan

110. **You don't have forever to do things, so do them now.**

— *Robert Stack*

111. **Looking at a situation through the other person's "glasses" reveals new perspectives.**

— *Sid Ridgley*

112. **Listen to the opposition.** Consider the conversations equivalent to the "six blind men describing an elephant." Each has a valid point of view.

— *Phoebe Bailey*

113. Rejection of new ideas is natural. Salespeople are taught to anticipate 99 *no's* to 1 *yes*. **When you are trying to win support for your new ideas, expect to hear a lot of *no's* on your way to finding the *yes's*.**

— *Doug Smart*

114. **To solve a challenge you are facing, get quiet.** Your inner voice will often speak to you in those quiet moments to give you the creative solutions you seek.

— *Cheryl Stock*

115. **When you present a problem, present three solutions along with it.** Victims identify problems. Victors identify solutions.

— *Keith L. Brown*

116. **If you can't think, go for a walk.** A change of atmosphere is good for you and gentle exercise helps shake up the brain cells.

— *Linda Edgecombe*

117. **Faced with a challenge, take a break and do something that makes you laugh.** Reflect on your childhood memories and find something funny. Before long, your challenge may not appear to be so bad after all.

— *Kafi Matimiloju*

118. **When attempting to solve a problem, think beyond yourself.** You probably have friends, business associates, and family members who have skills and abilities that can help in addressing your challenges. Consider what they can do to assist you as you consider how to address a situation.

— *Donna Satchell*

119. **Problems become *your* problems when you chose to accept them as such.** How often do people come to you saying, "We have a problem"? Sometimes others knowingly or unknowingly try to delegate their problems to you with that statement. Problem ownership should be a deliberate choice whenever possible.

— *Mike Monahan*

120. "Measure twice, cut once," is wisdom from my tailor.

— *Sid Ridgley*

121. Hurdles cease to be challenges when you jump over them.

— *Robert Stack*

122. **Don't complain about how things are going in your work environment.** Be an example of how they should be going and others will follow.

— *David G. Lewis*

123. When employees don't have trust in the leadership of an organization, employees feel reluctant to commit themselves.

— *Greg Maciolek*

124. To get the attention of a decision-maker, I mail a little shoe with a note in it that reads: "Now that I have one foot in the door let's talk about how I get the other one in."

— *DJ Harrington*

125. **Need a quick pick-me-up**? Pop some cinnamon gum in your mouth at work.

— *Mandi Stanley*

126. Welcome mistakes. **The more mistakes you make, the more you know what *not* to do in reaching the results you want.**

— *Phoebe Bailey*

127. **Do something to make a drudgery activity fun and mentally stimulating.** While cleaning the house, for example, put on a bathing suit, play some oldies tunes, and dance. Make up new words to familiar songs like *Happy Birthday* or *Jingle Bells* while mowing the lawn. Sing them aloud. This will take your mind off the drudgery of the cleaning or mowing because you will be having so much fun.

— *Cheryl Stock*

128. **Don't give your power away.** Stand firm against business bullies to develop your interpersonal leadership skills and move beyond daily struggles.

— *Connie Dieken*

129. **Plan to eliminate challenges that hold you back and cause you to get off track.**

— Kafi Matimiloju

130. **It is better to head off a problem than to have to fix one.** Preventative maintenance in areas under our control is essential. Be proactive rather than reactive.

— Mike Monahan

131. **Problem-oriented people create "pity parties." Solution-oriented people never want to get invited!**

— Keith L. Brown

132. **When it comes to change, twenty percent of people enjoy trying new things, fifty percent are on the fence until they decide if a change is good or bad, and thirty percent will instantly resist a change.** When voicing a new idea, a smart strategy is to first engage the support of the twenty percent. This will help you win over many of the fifty percent and strengthen your idea against the attacks of the thirty percent.

— Doug Smart

133. **Get past objections to new ideas by asking questions.** Uncover the other person's thinking.

— Sid Ridgley

134. **Discover the type of music that boosts your creativity and play it while you work.** Try various types, such as jazz, classical, hip-hop, etc., until you find the one that doesn't distract, but rather increases your creative output.

— Donna Satchell

135. **Creativity begins with the willingness to have a beginner's mind.**

— Robert Stack

136. **Reward creative input by giving credit where it is due.**

— Greg Maciolek

137. As you speak, you are perceived and you eventually become. **If you speak with confidence, you are perceived as confident, and you become more confident.** This lets people know you believe in what you are saying and doing, making it easier for them to believe in you, too.

— *Mandi Stanley*

138. **All commitments and promises made to clients have to be kept, otherwise the price to be paid is loss of trust, and that is always too high a price.**

— *DJ Harrington*

139. **Garden or spend time in another hobby that brings you peace.**

— *Linda Edgecombe*

140. **When you tackle challenges, you do more than** *understand.* **You begin to "overstand."** You can stand victorious over those challenges!

— *Keith L. Brown*

141. **Leaders are able to keep the big picture in focus while not losing sight of the small details.**

— *Cheryl Stock*

142. **A leader does not wait for permission to act.**

— *Phoebe Bailey*

143. **Make your culture idea-friendly.**
Encourage people around you to be candid
and you'll stop wasting time with cluttered,
cover-your-butt communications.
— *Connie Dieken*

144. **Overcome your challenge with enthusiasm**.
Take on your challenge with a good attitude.
Solving it will seem so much easier.
— *Kafi Matimiloju*

145. **Drink more—water that is!** The brain
is approximately 80% water. Research
has found that without an adequate level
of water in the body, the brain's electrical
activity is decreased, resulting in less
creative thinking. So before engaging in
creative endeavors, drink water.
— *Donna Satchell*

146. **When you slip into a slump, change your thinking quickly through reading powerful, positive literature that feeds your "can do" spirit.** An excellent book that has worked for me is *The Magic of Thinking Big* by Dr. David Schwartz.

— *Doug Smart*

147. **Problems that are ignored almost always get worse.** No matter how onerous, taking action is better than not taking action. Keep in mind:

- Take early action

- Don't be fooled by apparent self-cures

- Glue, bungee cords, and tape may not hold!

— *Mike Monahan*

148. Put a white board in your office to facilitate brainstorming and mind mapping. **Make it mandatory that everyone in your workplace add to the board one crazy or great idea each week.**

— *Linda Edgecombe*

149. *Turtling* **describes people coming out of their shells, snapping at others, and then returning to their shells.**

— *DJ Harrington*

150. **Ignore the pessimist that says it can't be done.**

— *Robert Stack*

151. **To date, no monument has ever been erected to honor nay-sayers.**
> — *David G. Lewis*

152. **Unless you are willing to change your thinking, you cannot grow.**
> — *Sid Ridgley*

153. **Push decision making down to the lowest level in order to help others grow.** Make the people on the front line responsible for themselves by empowering them to make decisions without having to ask permission.
> — *Greg Maciolek*

154. As a speaker and writer, **I keep an "idea journal" for each of my main topics and projects.** That way, I'm never at a loss for material. Here are some samples of what I'll add to my "idea journal": related articles, quotations, real-world examples from coworkers, funny stories I hear, brainstorms, illustrations, ideas for exercises, and sample visual aids.

— *Mandi Stanley*

155. **Nurture the child inside of you to boost your creativity.**

— *David G. Lewis*

156. **Grow your creativity by going the other way.** If your habitual inclination is to respond to a situation in a certain way, try doing the opposite and see what happens.

— *Cheryl Stock*

157. **Creative people tend to carve out their own roles rather than wait for assignments.**

— Phoebe Bailey

158. **Get off your duff at eighty percent.** When you're eighty percent done with a project, get moving toward a rapid completion. Don't hold out for "perfection."

— Connie Dieken

159. Happiness is ageless. **Don't let stressful life challenges prematurely age you.**

— Kafi Matimiloju

160. **Use the last 15 minutes of your business day to plan your next day.** This will give you a greater sense of control, drop stress, and open up creativity.

— Doug Smart

161. **When you stay open-minded and avoid jumping to conclusions, some challenges will end up in laughter.** On a recent flight, I politely spoke to the elegant, elderly woman next to me. No response. I asked if she was comfortable. Again, no response. This was a challenge. I thought she was a rude "Lemon Person" (negative), so I turned away and read a magazine. Five minutes later, she tapped me on the shoulder and asked, "Son, did you say something? My hearing aid needs new batteries." I burst out into laughter. I explained and she laughed too.

— *Keith L. Brown*

162. Effective problem solving requires a consistent and systematic process.

- Recognize a problem

- Accept it as yours to deal with

- Hypothesize the cause

- Do a rigorous analysis of the issues

- Accept divergent/convergent thinking

- Have alternative approaches

- Be willing to act

- Take action

- Measure results and adapt

— Mike Monahan

163. Talk to clever people and don't be afraid to disagree with them. **A stimulating argument can be a terrific way to give your brain cells a workout.** Important note: arguing about politics and film directors is good for you; bickering over who should clean the dishes is not.

— Linda Edgecombe

164. When workers are fully engaged, you realize greater productivity due to increased satisfaction, commitment, responsibility and lower frustration levels. **Further, you will find an increase in the quality of work, because the worker feels more like an "owner" or "partner."**

— Greg Maciolek

165. **Stress is the result of imbalance between work and personal lives.** If you find yourself stressed, ask one question: Will this matter five years from now? If yes, then do something about the situation. If not, then let it go.

— DJ Harrington

166. **Carry a small notebook and pen to jot down flashes of creative thoughts that come to you unexpectedly.** You want to capture creative ideas immediately because they have a tendency to dissipate as quickly as they appear.

— Donna Satchell

167. **Confidence is in the eye of the beholder.**
Follow the advice your mother gave you:
Stand up straight, make good eye contact,
smile—and don't forget to breathe!
— Mandi Stanley

168. **Undue worrying chokes the mind of its
ability to think clearly.**
— Sid Ridgley

169. **Play helps boost creativity.**
— Cheryl Stock

170. **Incorporate fun in all your projects.**
People are more creative when they are
having fun.
— David G. Lewis

171. **Being creative is the lifting of a person's vision to a higher plane of being.**
— *Robert Stack*

172. **Being creative allows you to turn challenges into opportunities.**
— *Phoebe Bailey*

173. **Getting started on a project opens up creativity.** If you find you procrastinate, start the first 5 minutes *now* and let momentum build.
— *Doug Smart*

174. **Do you deal with a narcissist?** This type blames, berates, and lobs grenades. Don't spin your wheels trying to change his behavior; his ego feeds on the conflict. It is better to focus on your own coping techniques and rise above his selfish, bullying behavior.

— Connie Dieken

175. **Get a "first class" mentality because "coach" is always overcrowded!**

— Keith L. Brown

176. **The quality of our answers is usually more important than our speed in answering.**

— Sid Ridgley

177. **Just as fire is vital for tempering steel, initial resistance to new ideas can be vital for transforming them from good to great.**

— Doug Smart

178. **Change with the times or be left behind!**
Things are constantly changing around us. Those who try to ignore the new by sticking with the old, risk becoming obsolete. Embrace change and grow. To resist change means to stay where you are — or even lose ground!

— Kafi Matimiloju

179. **Courage is having the mental strength to persevere. It does not mean having the solutions.**

— Sid Ridgley

180. Every solution has a risk. **The best decisions have less risk than that posed by the problem.**

— Mike Monahan

181. **Avoid "it has never been done before" thinking.** Just because somebody has not done something yet is no reason it cannot be accomplished. You might be the one to sidestep previous obstacles such as inexperience, poor timing, lack of knowledge, deficient skills, limited relationships, and shaky commitment. Each individual is unique. Your participation will bring to bear your own special skills, abilities, connections, and traits that can make the winning difference.

— Donna Satchell

182. **The best solution to a challenge may not be the most obvious one.**

— Robert Stack

183. **Transforming your thinking is the first step towards transforming your world.**

— Sid Ridgley

184. Ever notice how tough it is to formulate sentences after you've come off a good vacation. **Our minds need some tough challenges to keep them sharp.**

— Linda Edgecombe

185. **Be a giver.** In the long run, giving to others always comes back to the giver.

— Greg Maciolek

186. **Overcome communication challenges with your ABCs: Make your message *Accurate, Brief,* and *Clear.***

— *Mandi Stanley*

187. **Being creative means being free to think outside the box.**

— *David G. Lewis*

188. **A sure way to boost your creativity is to make a five-year old your guru.** The child's thought process will show you how to think in new ways.

— *Phoebe Bailey*

189. **Carry index cards in your car or briefcase.** They are perfect for ideas and brainstorms, many of which come during a drive across town. These will not get lost as easily as stray pieces of paper. Also, if you collect a number of ideas around a project or situation, you can organize your thoughts by sorting your cards.

— Cheryl Stock

190. Stress is caused by the knowledge I am not doing what I know I need to be doing in order to be successful. **So do the things you know you need to be doing, even if you don't feel like doing them.**

— Doug Smart

191. **De-stress yourself by turning your stress into energy!** When times are tough, take yourself away from the situation at hand. Participate in your favorite physical activity, like walking, dancing, and swimming. Funnel your stress into re-energizing yourself.

— *Kafi Matimiloju*

192. **Have high expectations for yourself.** No one rises to low expectations.

— *Keith L. Brown*

193. **Management recognition of the importance of personal and family life is a major factor in maintaining employee respect and loyalty.**

— *DJ Harrington*

194. **Are you a thinker?** Are you analytical, detail-oriented and process-oriented? You'll spark your creativity by concentrating on one thing at a time. Use a logical, step-by-step manner and then implement, implement, implement.

— *Connie Dieken*

195. **To stimulate creative thinking in an organization or on a team, reward creative ideas.** People like appreciation for their efforts. When people realize they will receive recognition or tangibles that are meaningful to them, ideas flow faster.

— *Donna Satchell*

196. Bring a healthy plant into your workspace. **A plant will bring life into your workspace and will also absorb toxins in the air.**

— Linda Edgecombe

197. **To feel more alert, put some eucalyptus branches in your work area and inhale their energizing scent.**

— Mandi Stanley

198. **If you are the boss, stop thinking that promoting someone to supervisor is the best way to reward top performing people.** It is not a reward if the individual does not have a skill set for supervision.

— Greg Maciolek

199. **If you can't change it, try celebrating it!**
In my military career, I had the opportunity
to serve several tours with the Marine
Corps. The Marine Corps gets the toughest
assignments and hand-me-down equipment
but has developed a sense of pride in their
condition that enhances morale and helps
them be successful.

— Mike Monahan

200. **Play with words, thoughts, and colors
to stimulate your creativity.** Move them
around, stir them up, use puns, be corny,
capture your thoughts in different colors
of ink.

— Cheryl Stock

201. In working on a team, alignment is more important than agreement.

— *Phoebe Bailey*

202. Every day, get out of bed and clap! May it be your first standing ovation of the day!

— *Keith L. Brown*

203. Sometimes simply changing the focus changes the outcome.

— *Robert Stack*

204. Changing your thinking is as important as changing your clothes.

— *Sid Ridgley*

205. **Intelligent meetings spark creativity.**
Meetings with clear agendas and objectives
produce the best ideas, plans and decisions.
Don't let human crosscurrents sweep
discussions off course.

— Connie Dieken

206. When it comes to tasks and projects, stop
following everyone else. Robert Frost wrote,
"Two roads diverged in a wood, and I— I
took the one less traveled by, And that has
made all the difference." **Create new paths
and leave a trail for others to follow.**

— Keith L. Brown

207. **Barriers are always present in a changing
environment**. Capture energy around the
barrier or conflict and turn it into a positive
force to break down the barrier.

— Kafi Matimiloju

208. **Influence is more important than force.**
— *Phoebe Bailey*

209. **Embrace the thought that the challenge you are facing has more than one solution.** Many times we limit our thinking because we stop when we come up with one workable answer. Realize that most challenges have multiple solutions.
— *Donna Satchell*

210. When tried and true isn't, remember the formula: OM≠NR. **This formula is "Old Methods do not equal New Results."** It is a reminder that new methods may nccd to be developed in order to get new results.
— *Mike Monahan*

211. **Just like a gardener, we have to prune the negative thoughts in our minds.**

— Sid Ridgley

212. **Negative thinking closes the mind like shuttering a house before a storm. Positive thinking opens the mind to welcome bright, new possibilities.**

— Doug Smart

213. **To boost the creativity of a team, suspend judgments about any ideas presented until decision-making is necessary.** Nothing stops creativity faster than passing judgment on ideas during brainstorming. Resist this tendency.

— Donna Satchell

214. **Learn to think outside the box and you'll
never be boxed in.**

— Robert Stack

215. **If you're living on the edge, you're
taking up too much space! Leap and face
challenges with creativity and enthusiasm!**

— Keith L. Brown

216. **View each challenge as an opportunity
to grow instead of a stumbling block.**
Whenever you're faced with a challenge,
choose to be optimistic. Assess the situation,
avoid worry, and look for the positive.

— David G. Lewis

217. How do you drive a turtle down the road? He's overly cautious and slow to make a decision because he's afraid he'll make the wrong move. **To move a turtle, give him two or three choices so he doesn't feel that the weight of the world rides on him.**
— *Connie Dieken*

218. **Success starts with a single thought: "I can."**
— *Sid Ridgley*

219. **Clutter is like emotional constipation - it bogs you down.** Filing cabinets need to be regularly purged and desktops kept clutter free. How is your inbox? If you see hundreds of emails when you open your inbox you will feel overwhelmed. Delete emails no longer needed.
— *Linda Edgecombe*

220. **Many people who quit, quit their supervisors, not the company.**

— *Greg Maciolek*

221. **Your best and brightest ideas don't always come to you while at work.** Be prepared. Sometimes you are in the least opportune places when hit with sudden strokes of brilliance! These places include:

- Commuting, stuck in traffic

- Showering, getting dressed

- Sleeping, lying in bed

- Exercising, performing a routine activity

— *Mandi Stanley*

222. **In order to become more creative, develop the characteristics of creative individuals.** They are curious, observant, questioning, imaginative, positive, open, and receptive.

— Donna Satchell

223. **Creative idea: To get the attention of a prospect, mail socks and tell the prospect you will "knock their socks off."**

— DJ Harrington

224. **Celebrate your successes, big and small.** Celebrations give you momentum to do more.

— Cheryl Stock

225. **Celebrate the results associated with conquering your challenges.** Enjoy the pleasure and satisfaction that comes with overcoming a challenge. Learn from the experience and celebrate your success.

— Kafi Matimiloju

226. **Take classes or engage in activities that will utilize your creative abilities.** Such activities include painting, poetry-writing, journaling, sculpting, and cabinet making.

— Donna Satchell

227. **To get new results, you need new inputs.** Reading, taking a class, talking with someone who is creative and positive will help you shift your thinking. This is especially helpful when you are in a rut.

— Doug Smart

228. **How you think about a situation or a relationship, very much determines how you will respond to it.**

— *Sid Ridgley*

229. **By consciously creating your environment, your environment will in turn create a quality of life to support you in reaching your potential.** Feng Shui has a powerful effect in your life and you can use these enhancements to create a flow of prosperity, energy and creativity in your work life.

— *Linda Edgecombe*

230. **Improve your batting average.** Learn from yesterday and implement today as if your life depends on it. It does.

— Connie Dieken

231. **If you're the most creative person in your group of influence then you need to find another group.**

— David G. Lewis

232. **I wear a link on my belt loop to symbolize this: I can be the missing link, the weak link, or the link to success.**

— DJ Harrington

233. **Your ability to comeback from adversity requires only one thing . . . you.**

— Robert Stack

234. **The best fix lasts forever.** Problems have a tendency to reoccur with increasing frequency and severity unless the underlying issues are addressed. Some tools to consider are:

• Root problem analysis

• Process improvement opportunities

• Divorce versus separation: do you want to deal with it or do away with it.

— *Mike Monahan*

235. **Give yourself permission to dream.** Pretend you have a magic wand and are waving it over your life. Fantasize about what your life would be like if the obstacles in your path were removed or minimized. If you like the possibilities, set your creative energies and come up with ways to deal with the obstacles.

— *Cheryl Stock*

236. **Workers need to feel appreciated and that their work matters.** They need to feel a sense of accomplishment and fulfillment.

— *Greg Maciolek*

237. Feeling weary on a warm day? **Run a cold can along your neck and forehead for an instant revival.**

— *Mandi Stanley*

238. **Study the most creative people you know and observe their habits and how they spend their time.**

— *Phoebe Bailey*

239. **Solving problems leads to improvements**. Many of us view problems as roadblocks. We agonize over them and then allow them to set us back. Embrace your problems and attack them with a vengeance. What you learn from the experience will strengthen and develop your life skills.

— *Kafi Matimiloju*

240. **Turn stumbling blocks into stepping stones.**

— *Keith L. Brown*

241. **Keep a "smart journal" in your car, beside your bed, and in your kitchen.** When brilliant ideas enter your life, immediately write them down in the journal that's physically closest to you. Review your smart journals once a week to implement ideas.

— *Connie Dieken*

242. **To develop and maintain an attitude of creativity, try two new things every day.** These can be simple, such as going to work by a different route, eating something new for lunch, or starting a conversation with a stranger.

— *Doug Smart*

243. **To boost the creativity of a team, temporarily suspend status of team members.** This means relinquishing titles and placing all members on the same level during a brainstorming session. In this environment, lower level members can feel their ideas have an equal chance of being heard and considered as those of members in upper level positions. Creativity flourishes in such an atmosphere.

— *Donna Satchell*

244. Symptoms only look like the problem.
Effective problem-solving requires a willingness to look for root causes and avoid the "Ladder of Inference" — using assumptions rather than data to take you to conclusions that might not be valid although they seem logical.

— Mike Monahan

245. **As a leader, your people have to see that your actions are not motivated by your ego, but by your desire to have them give their best.**

— Sid Ridgley

246. **Brushing your teeth or combing your hair with the non-dominant hand uses brain synapses that are less frequently used.** This is an easy way to give them a "work out."

— *Cheryl Stock*

247. Need some instant energy to overcome an afternoon lull? **Brush your teeth and then gargle with a powerful minty mouthwash after lunch.** In fact, I carry an extra toothbrush wherever I go!

— *Mandi Stanley*

248. The mind is likely to get in gear in certain environments. **Have a place reserved exclusively for creative thought, such as a park bench or a special room.**

— *Phoebe Bailey*

249. When you have an issue that appears to be "impossible" to solve, you are at an impasse. **Some effective approaches for dealing with impasses include:**

- Work on other issues and set aside the difficult issue for now, all the time knowing your sub-conscious is still working on the impasse.

- Find a way to minimize the impact of the tough issue so a solution may be reached.
  — *Mike Monahan*

250. **Life's whispered teachings come in the form of wake-up calls.**
— *Robert Stack*

251. **Overcoming challenges and achieving more requires thinking with your heart in it.**
— *Sid Ridgley*

252. **Your intuition is your internal tool for perceiving any situation.** Become more aware of what's going on in your body. Some people call this being more present in all situations. When something just doesn't sit well with you, your senses are trying to tell you something.

— *Linda Edgecombe*

253. **Never be afraid to question the status quo.** Every great invention or discovery started with someone asking the simple question, "why not?"

— *David G. Lewis*

254. **Let them know you know.** To encourage others' contributions, communicate two things: awareness (*You did a great job!*) and appreciation. (*Thanks for your contribution.*)

— *Connie Dieken*

255. **When the going gets tough, focus on the light at the end of the tunnel rather than the immediate difficulties.** That light will shine brighter as things get better.

— Kafi Matimiloju

256. **Dwell with those who are smarter than you by asking for help.**

— Keith L. Brown

257. **Work in a career that is a fit for your personal interests, attitudes, and values.** This may seem obvious, but studies continue to show that approximately fifty percent of North Americans rate their job satisfaction between unhappy and miserable. It is hard to be creative if you feel mired in a job you dislike.

— Doug Smart

258. **Numerous studies confirm that workers want challenging work, a company that cares about them, the feeling that they are "in on things," and appreciation for making a difference.** Pay and benefits are always lower down the list.

— *Greg Maciolek*

259. Imagine a buffet with only one meat, one vegetable, one dessert, and one beverage. Boring! **Craft your daily tasks like a well designed buffet — and heaps of variety and choices.**

— *Keith L. Brown*

260. **Great ideas often fail because we fail to think through the challenges of implementation.** If detail work is not a natural strength of yours, develop support teams.

— *Sid Ridgley*

261. **We are most effective in solving problems in areas in which we have control**. We have limited energy, time and influence. Focusing on those problems that directly affect us increases the likelihood that we will be successful problem solvers and will actually increase our influence in other areas. Also, this approach gains us a reputation as a person who gets it done.
— *Mike Monahan*

262. **When presenting solutions to problems, don't present more than two or three viable ones.** Any more than that confuses the mind of the decision-maker. And a confused mind finds it simpler to say "no."
— *Sid Ridgley*

263. **If you are working inside and find that your creative juices are not flowing, go outside and spend some quiet time in the woods, a park, or by a lake.** Many people find the tranquility of nature to be a creativity stimulus.

— *Donna Satchell*

264. **The world's most creative people wander where there is no path**.

— *DJ Harrington*

265. **Work-life balance is a deal you make with yourself.** Balance means making choices and implementing them. Only you know the trade-offs you're willing to make. Many people struggle with the logistics. Instead, clarify the outcomes you want from balance and say "no" to things that don't fit.

— *Connie Dieken*

266. **Rev your engine.** Clarify your goals down to the nitty-gritty to ensure your life runs more efficiently.

— Connie Dieken

267. **I challenge you to challenge you!**

— Keith L. Brown

268. **Creative idea: I carry pacifiers on strings in case I come across people who whine.**

— DJ Harrington

269. **Dare to be you! What do you have to lose?** Make a bold statement by taking the risk to do something that you've always wanted to do.

— David G. Lewis

270. **Knowledge tempered with wisdom is a good start. However, without understanding, it's useless.**

— David G. Lewis

271. **Maintain an attitude of gratitude.** It is impossible to be grateful and depressed simultaneously.

— Doug Smart

272. **Be sure to thank people who have helped you.**

— Mandi Stanley

273. **Positive attitudes promote creative thinking, but negative ones can hold you back**. To help solve difficult challenges, form your own inner circle of friends to help you brainstorm solutions. Build your inner circle with those who have positive and optimistic attitudes towards helping you resolve challenges. Anyone (including you) with a negative attitude will undermine your thinking process and, in turn, will limit your results.

— Kafi Matimiloju

274. **Giving people a choice is a powerful motivator.**

— Sid Ridgley

275. **Sometimes the simplest things can give creativity a big boost.** Indulge! When I suffer from "writer's block," I doodle with colorful scented markers.

— Mandi Stanley

276. **Creative people won't put up with being micro-managed.**

— Greg Maciolek

277. **Create a story board or holiday greeting card with pictures and words cut out of magazines.** This is a fun way to challenge your mind to create in an unconventional way.

— Cheryl Stock

278. **Don't blow hot air.** Most visions and
values are hot air that no one really believes.
Tie your goals to real actions so you'll know
when you've reached them.

— *Connie Dieken*

279. **Start with a simple task which requires
you to improvise and work your way to
something more complex, such as cooking
without a recipe, arranging flowers, or
decorating a room.**

— *Phoebe Bailey*

280. Clear the clutter in your home and office.
Clutter is anything unfinished, unused,
unresolved, tolerated or disorganized.
**When you clear your clutter, your energy
and creativity increase.**

— *Linda Edgecombe*

281. Keep paper and pen next to your bed so you can capture the creative ideas that swirl around in your head just before you go to sleep and just after you wake up.

— Doug Smart

282. Attitudes cannot be bought but they can be created.

— Sid Ridgley

283. Keep hydrated by drinking plenty of water at work.

— Mandi Stanley

284. **The most difficult problems to manage are those involving other people.** To manage problems involving people, one must have an understanding of human nature, a commitment to win-win and tolerance for compromise.

— *Mike Monahan*

285. **Bring more brains into the game**. Create an open environment so people feel free to be candid and creative, instead of being courteously remote.

— *Connie Dieken*

286. **Look for something positive in everything in your life, even setbacks.** The purpose is to keep your mind open to using the lessons you learn in life, especially the hard lessons.

— *Doug Smart*

287. **A challenge is a solution before the question has been asked.**

— *David G. Lewis*

288. **As a leader, take the time to link small actions with the bigger picture. This will raise the self-esteem and confidence of those you lead.**

— *Sid Ridgley*

289. As Dolly Parton said in *Steel Magnolias*: **"Smile, Honey. It increases your face value."**

— *Mandi Stanley*

290. Any time you feel the urge to give up, visit a grave yard. **If you're still breathing, you still have hope!**

— *Keith L. Brown*

291. **Put together gift baskets for friends and family by color themes.** An example could be an "Orange you glad it's fall" basket filled with things that are orange. Some possibilities could be autumn leaves, orange blossom honey, orange flavored cookies and herbal teas.

— Cheryl Stock

292. **Challenges help you discover things about yourself and are part of everyone's growth process.**

— Sid Ridgley

293. **Shift gears and gain a competitive advantage**. Rather than seeing yourself as a person who reacts to change, in some situations, see yourself as a driver of change in order to be competitive.

— Kafi Matimiloju

294. Creative idea: When people say, "I want to sleep on it" before making a decision, I take out a pillow case with my company name on it and give it to them.

— *DJ Harrington*

295. Surround yourself with music, community, and conversation as a means to opening your mind.

— *Phoebe Bailey*

296. Build creativity and confidence by treating your employees like you want them to treat your best customer.

— *Greg Maciolek*

297. Release the need to always be right and learn to accept things as they are.

— *Robert Stack*

298. **Don't expect to live problem free.**
We thrive on a moderately resistive
environment. Our life situations are like
muscle groups: Problem solving is like
"exercise" that strengthens our ability to
deal with problems. People who have it
too easy don't do well when problems
occur and may feel worn down by life.
Take advantage of your challenges to grow
stronger.

— Mike Monahan

299. **Boost your creative thinking by
considering unconventional uses for
an item.** An example would be milk jugs
shredded to make fabric.

— Donna Satchell

300. **How you respond to a negative experience shows your character.**

— *Sid Ridgley*

301. **Let your creative juices flow**. For many people, disorganization is part of their creative process. If this is you, while your creative ideas are flowing, capture your thoughts on paper, video, or recording device and organize them later.

— *Kafi Matimiloju*

302. **Here are some probing questions to consider when taking a creative approach to problem solving.**

- What is the problem?

- By solving this issue, what will I gain?

- What will I have to let go of?

- Is it my problem? What's in it for me?

- Can I delegate it to someone else?

- Can I solve it? Is it worth solving?

- Is this the real problem, or merely a symptom of a larger one?

- If this is an old problem, what's wrong with the previous solution?

- Is there a pattern to how this problem is presenting itself?

- Does it need an immediate solution, or can it wait?

- Is it likely to go away by itself?

- Can I risk ignoring it?

- Does the problem have ethical dimensions?

- How will I celebrate when I solve this problem?

— Linda Edgecombe

303. **When people go home at night, they want to say, "I made a difference today."**

— Greg Maciolek

"The problems of the world cannot possibly be solved by skeptics or cynics whose horizons are limited by the obvious realities. We need men who can dream of things that never were."

— John F. Kennedy

"The whole of science is nothing more than a refinement of everyday thinking."

— Albert Einstein

*"There are no days in life
so memorable as
those which vibrated
to some stroke
of the imagination."*

— Ralph Waldo Emerson

*"There is nothing
that cannot be achieved by
firm imagination."*

— Japanese proverb

Contributors

Phoebe Bailey

Through motivational speeches, seminars and workshops, Phoebe moves audiences from theory to practice in building community, increasing effectiveness, and recapturing the joy of a life committed to growth and development. Her messages reflect the hard lessons learned on the frontline as teacher, trainer, and public school administrator.

Contact Information:
Phoebe L. Bailey, Ph.D.
Visions in Action USA
955 Juniper Street NE, Suite 4130
Atlanta, GA 30309
Phone: (404) 892-9066
E-mail: drbailey@VisionsInActionUSA.com
Website: www.VisionsInActionUSA.com

CSP, *Certified Speaking Professional*, is the highest earned designation of the National Speakers Association.

Keith L. Brown

Called the "Motivator of the Millennium," Keith helps people move from living under supervision to manifesting a SUPER-VISION. His keynotes and workshops inspire and empower education, corporate, government, and faith-based organizations. Keith is the author of *CHITLINS [Creative Helpful Intuitive Thoughts Lifting Individuals Naturally Seeking]* and co-author of *Conversations on Success*. He and his lovely wife, Wakea, are proud parents of one sensational son, Keon.

Contact Information:
Keith L. Brown
20/20 Enterprises
115 Courtney's Lane
Fayetteville, GA 30215
Phone: (770) 460-5679
Toll-free: (800) 725-2694, pin 0726
E-mail: KeithSpeaks@KeithLBrown.com
Website: www.KeithLBrown.com

Linda Edgecombe, CSP

Linda is an internationally known humorous speaker, trainer and consultant. The *Wall Street Journal* has quoted her as an expert on shifting perspectives. Linda shows audiences how they can shift their perspectives on life, work and themselves. Her message is as welcome as a deep belly laugh and as profound as an honest look in the mirror.

Contact Information:
Linda Edgecombe, CSP
Learning Edge Resources
2770 Reyn Road
Kelowna, British Columbia V1V 2G7
Phone: (250) 868-9601
Toll-free: (888) 868-9601
E-mail: LindaEdgecombe@shaw.ca
Website: www.LindaEdgecombe.com

Connie Dieken

Connie Dieken helps organizations build buy-in through influential communication. She is a 5-time Emmy® Award winner and inductee in the Radio & Television Broadcasters Hall of Fame. Connie teaches how to cut through CommuniClutter™ with clarity, and influence customers and staff to trigger commitment and powerful results. She is a co-author of *Communicate Clearly, Confidently & Credibly*.

Contact Information:
Connie Dieken
onPoint™ Communication
32818 Walker Road, #298
Avon Lake, OH 44012
Phone: (440) 930-8500
Toll-free: (800) 505-9480
E-mail: Connie@onPointComm.com
Website: www.onPointComm.com

DJ Harrington, CSP

DJ has provided companies worldwide with marketing and telephone skills designed to enhance their telephone and customer service techniques. He teaches the EMS formula for guaranteed success: *educate*, *motivate*, and carry *solutions*. He is a nationally recognized author, journalist, seminar leader and marketing consultant.

Contact Information:
DJ Harrington, CSP
Phone Logic, Inc.
2189 Cleveland Street, Suite 257
Clearwater, FL 33765
Toll-free: (800) 352-5252
E-mail: DJHarrington@tune2.tv

David G. Lewis

David is an energetic speaker who uses his personal experience to motivate and teach people how to make sense of a world that often seems senseless. He speaks at conferences and conventions across North America. He teaches Political Science at Heartland College.

Contact Information:
David G. Lewis
Lewis Consulting Group, Inc.
1701 E. Empire Street, Suite 360 #146
Bloomington, IL 61704
Phone: (309) 827-0540
E-mail: David@DavidGLewis.com
Website: www.DavidGLewis.com

Greg Maciolek

As a consultant and speaker, Greg helps organizations increase profits by increasing productivity and decreasing employee turnover. He does this through leadership development at the senior level and working with executive teams to be more effective. He uses employee assessments for hiring, promoting and developing employees. He has served as a fighter pilot and flying commander responsible for 1,100 members.

Contact Information:
Greg Maciolek
Integrated Management Resources, Inc.
P.O. Box 31933
Knoxville, TN 37930-1933
Phone: (865) 539-3700
Toll-free: (800) 262-6403
E-mail: Greg.Maciolek@imrtn.com
Website: www.IntegratedManagementResources.com

Kafi Matimiloju

An international speaker, trainer, and consultant, Kafi has spent sixteen years working with Fortune 1000 organizations supporting projects that require the successful integration of people, processes and technology. Formerly a shy and reserved business professional who loathed networking, Kafi beat her fear and now enjoys power networking. Her motto, "Be memorable and leave a lasting impression!" Kafi leads self-improvement seminars that are interactive, informative, and fun.

Contact Information:
Kafi Matimiloju
KiSoBo, Inc.
P.O. Box 19957
Atlanta, GA 30325
Phone: (678) 797-0369
E-mail: Kafi@KiSoBo.com
Website: www.KiSoBo.com

Mike Monahan

Mike's expertise is in helping teams and individuals improve performance, with special focus on the human side of change. Mike conducts leader and manager competency development sessions and has a series of customizable training interventions for all levels of supervisors and managers. He is a co-author of *Where There's Change There's Opportunity, Irresistible Leadership, Thriving in the Midst of Change,* and all six volumes of the *Insights from Experts* Series.

Contact Information:
Mike Monahan
Healthcare Resources Associates
8505 S. Newcombe Court, Suite A
Littleton, CO 80127
Phone and Fax: (303) 948-1587
Toll-free: (800) 759-2881
E-mail: M2HRA@aol.com

Sid Ridgley, CSP

As an organizational development specialist and professional speaker, Sid advises leaders in their pursuit of creating organizational workplaces that are customer and employee centered. His areas of expertise are customer satisfaction and loyalty, sales, leadership development, and front-line driven cultural change processes.

Contact Information:
Sid Ridgley, MBA, CSP
Simul Corporation
23 Fry Court
Markham, Ontario L3P 4G9
Phone: (905) 294-1260
Toll-free: (888) 291-7892
E-mail: SRidgley@SimulCorp.com
Website: www.SimulCorp.com

Donna Satchell

Donna works with individuals who want to achieve remarkable success and businesses that want strong teams that serve their customers exceptionally well. In addition, she teaches public speaking skills. Her company name, STARR is an acronym for Speeches, Training, Assessments, Resources and Results, which are the deliverables her business provides across North America.

Contact Information:
Donna Satchell
STARR Consulting & Training LLC
6304 Southland Forest Drive
Stone Mountain, GA 30087
Phone: (770) 498-0400
E-mail: Donna@STARRct.com
Website: www.STARRct.com

Doug Smart , CSP

Doug Smart helps people work smart and live happy. He has expertise in helping organizations select, develop, and retain top talent. He is the author of the book, *Sell Smarter, Faster & Easier by Understanding Your Buyer's Personality Profile*. Doug is frequently invited to speak at conferences and conventions.

Contact Information:
Doug Smart, CSP
Smart Business, Inc.
PO Box 768024
Roswell, GA 30076
Phone: (770) 587-9784
Toll-free: (800) 299-3737
E-mail: Doug@DougSmart.com
Website: www.DougSmart.com

Robert Stack

As a professional development coach, Robert is dedicated to improving the quality of life for others who face life's not so funny stuff. He specializes in personal reputation management and coaches individuals as well as organizations on how to transform adversity into opportunity. He is co-author of *Success is a Journey*.

Contact Information:
Robert Stack, CLC, APR, Fellow PRSA
COMEBACK LLC
4521 PGA Blvd.
Palm Beach Gardens, FL 33418
Phone: (561) 776-0101
Toll-free: (866) 666-6064
E-mail: Robert@ComebackCoach.com
Website: www.ComebackCoach.com

Cheryl Stock

Cheryl works with people who want more energy, direction and passion in their lives and results from their businesses. Her expertise is in communication and presentation skills, marketing, leadership and achieving higher accomplishment levels. In 2003, Cheryl was named "Trainer of the Year" by the Non-Profit Resource Center. As one client says, "She'll rock you with her energy. She is contagious!"

Contact Information:
Cheryl Stock
C. Stock & Associates, Inc.
P.O. Box 25355
Sarasota, FL 34277
Phone: (941) 346-3624
E-mail: Cheryl@CherylStock.com
Website: www.CherylStock.com

Mandi Stanley, CSP

Mandi works with business leaders who want to boost their professional image and with people who want to be better speakers and writers. Her signature seminars are *"Hair-On-Fire!" Presentation Skills, 7½ Ways To Wake Up Your Writing,* and *Proof It: How To Be A Better Proofreader.* All are designed to help participants get their messages across and achieve the results they want.

Contact Information:
Mandi Stanley, CSP
429 Cherry Hill Drive
Madison, MS 39110
Phone: (601) 856-8282
E-mail: Mandi@MandiStanley.com
Website:www.MandiStanley.com